Betwee

Writter

MW01706446

CONTENTS

PEARSON

Between the Flags

When summer arrives and the weather turns warm, people often plan a day at the beach for a bit of fun in the sun and a swim or surf. But fun and water anywhere, particularly at a beach, can be a deadly mix and can very quickly turn into tragedy.

The ocean is a dangerous and powerful force that can be unpredictable from one minute to the next. If a person gets into trouble in the ocean and does not know what to do, drowning can be a real danger. Luckily, a lot of beaches have 'eyes'. These 'eyes' are the lifeguards and surf lifesavers that look after peoples' safety at the beach.

The lifeguards and surf lifesavers guarding the beach constantly scan the surf, watching everybody and keeping an eye out for warning signs of impending disaster. They know exactly what to do in a dangerous situation and how to handle a swimmer or surfer who is in trouble in the water. They save and protect the lives of people every day all over the world.

Lifeguards watching swimmers in the surf

Lifeguards patrolling the sea

Patrolling the Beach

Lifeguards and surf lifesavers do the same job. The only difference is that lifeguards are paid, whereas surf lifesavers are volunteers who give up their time without being paid.

Some lifeguards patrol the beach using quad bikes.

You will often see lifeguards or surf lifesavers sitting in chairs or towers high above the beach where they can view the ocean far away as well as up close. They also patrol by foot or drive up and down the beach using quad bikes and off-road vehicles. Sometimes they can even be up in the air in helicopters or planes, depending on how much beach and ocean they have to watch.

Lifeguards sit in towers to watch the beach.

Understanding the Beach and Ocean

Most beachgoers have no idea of the many dangerous unknowns that form part of a visit to the beach. Because of this, lifeguards and surf lifesavers need to know their patch of beach and surf thoroughly. They know that one of the greatest dangers to any person swimming in the ocean is a rip current.

A rip current, also known as a rip, is a strong current of water that starts at the shore and flows away from the beach, or runs parallel to the beach before heading out into the ocean.

Warning sign at a beach

When people get caught up in a rip current, most don't know what to do or how to cope. They often panic and get swept out into the ocean, where drowning can be a quick and silent death. It is estimated that, in Australia, 90 per cent of beach rescues and 40 per cent of drowning deaths are caused by rip currents.

Lifeguards and surf lifesavers know where rips occur on the beaches they patrol and they are able to recognise drowning people by watching out for certain behaviours. They are also extremely fit and very strong swimmers.

If you get caught in a rip current:

1. Don't panic. Keep calm and don't struggle against the current or you will use up all your energy.
2. Try to swim parallel to the beach to move out of the rip current. Then the waves will help you get back to the shore.
3. If you can't swim out of the rip current, float or calmly tread water. When out of the current, swim towards the beach.
4. If you still can't get to the shore, draw attention to yourself. Raise one arm for help.

Rescue Equipment

When performing a rescue in the ocean, a lifeguard or surf lifesaver uses special equipment.

Depending on how rough the ocean is, this equipment can be:

- a rescue tube or board;
- an inflatable rescue boat;
- a long surfboard;
- a jet ski.

If lifeguards and surf lifesavers need to rescue somebody, they will often swim out into the surf with a rescue tube or long surfboard.

Long surfboard and rescue belt

Inflatable rescue boat

The tube is buoyant and allows a person in danger of drowning to grab onto it while being pulled back to shore by the lifeguard. A long surfboard can be used in the same way. The tube and surfboard also help protect the lifeguards. Often when the lifeguards are performing a rescue, the person in danger of drowning is panicking. If the tubes or surfboards were not there, the lifeguards risk being pulled under the water and could drown, too.

When the ocean is rough and conditions are dangerous for lifeguards to swim in, an inflatable rescue boat or jet ski is used. They can easily traverse large waves and very quickly reach a person who is in danger.

A lifeguard on a jet ski can quickly reach a swimmer in trouble.

Rescue Training

Lifeguards and surf lifesavers receive training in many areas. These include:

- training in safety of the public,
- training in beach management,
- training in rescue techniques,
- training in first aid,
- training in resuscitation techniques (CPR).

If a person who has been rescued from the water is unconscious and has stopped breathing, a lifeguard or surf lifesaver will perform CPR. By using this technique, they are often able to revive a person and return them to consciousness — thereby saving their life.

Volunteers learning CPR training

How to Perform CPR

STEP 1

Call emergency service.

STEP 2

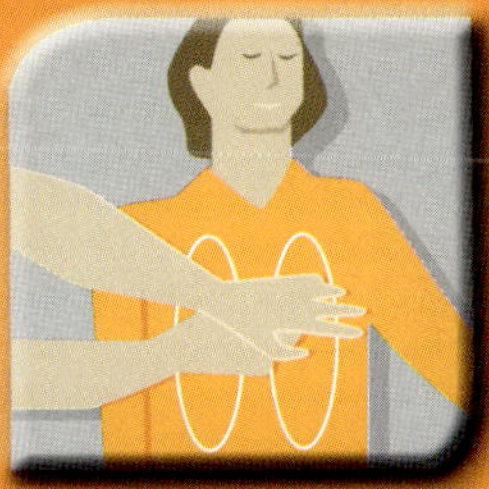

Position hands in the centre of the chest.

STEP 3

Tilt head, lift chin, check breathing.

STEP 4

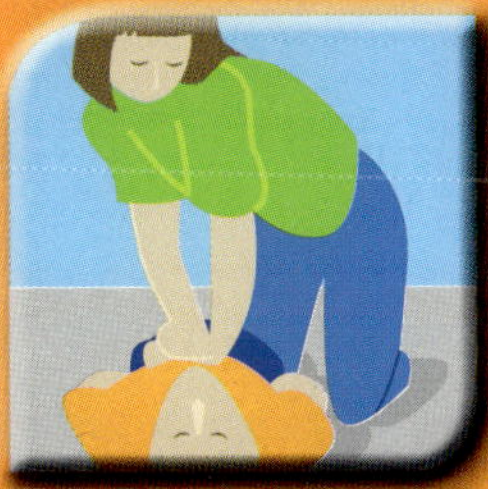

Firmly push down two inches on the chest 30 times.

STEP 5

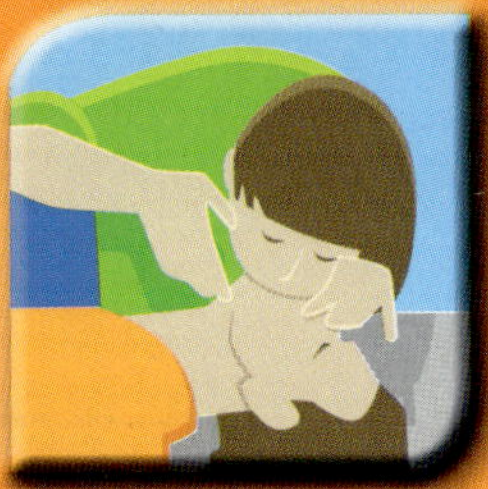

Give two breaths.

Continue with two breaths and 30 pumps until help arrives.

These lifeguards are doing a rescue exercise. They are holding the man's neck so it will not be damaged.

Keeping Safe in the Ocean

People need to understand that they are also responsible for their own safety at the beach and in the ocean. It only takes a few seconds for any swimmer or surfer to get into trouble in the water, panic and drown.

By following a few simple rules, tragedy can easily be avoided.

- Don't swim at a beach that is closed or where there are no lifeguards or surf lifesavers on duty.
- Ask a lifeguard/surf lifesaver for safety information before swimming.
- Read the safety and information signs before swimming.

Some warning signs you may see at a beach

Always swim between the red and yellow flags.

- Always swim between the red and yellow flags. This is the safe swim zone.
- Never swim alone. If you swim with a friend, you can watch over each other.
- Do not swim in deep water if you are not a confident swimmer.
- If you get caught in a rip current, do not struggle against it. Try to swim with it.
- If you need help, stay calm and raise your arm in the air to get the attention of a lifeguard.

Even though lifeguards and surf lifesavers are constantly on the lookout, people still drown every day.

When people are at the beach they should find the red and yellow flags and always swim between them. If a lifeguard or surf lifesaver can't see them, they can't save them.

Index

Informational Reports

Informational Reports record factual information about a specific topic

How to Write an Informational Report

Step One

- Select a topic.
- Write down the things you know about the topic.
- Write down the things you need to find out.

Between the Flags
– Research Brief

- Why do people get into trouble in the water?
- What do lifeguards and lifesavers do to protect people?
- What helps them spot people in trouble?
- What do they need to know about the beach/ocean?
- What can people do if they are caught in a rip?
- What equipment do lifeguards and lifesavers need?
- What training do they need?
- What can people do to keep themselves safe in the water?

Step Two

- Locate the information you need.
- Use different kinds of resources for your investigation:

Internet
Library
Television
Documentaries
Experts...

- Take notes or make copies of what you find.

Step Three

- Sort through your notes.
- Organise your information using headings.

Rescue Equipment
Lifeguards need special equipment

- Rescue tube or board for people to grab and be towed in
- Long surfboard – used for same
- Inflatable rescue boat – used in rough sea to get to drowning person quickly
- Jet ski – to get to drowning person quickly

Step Four

- Use your notes to write your Report.
- Include an **introduction** with an opening statement:

The ocean is a dangerous and powerful force that can be unpredictable from one minute to the next. If a person gets into trouble in the ocean and does not know what to do, drowning can be a real danger. Luckily, a lot of beaches have 'eyes'. These 'eyes' are the lifeguards and surf lifesavers that look after peoples' safety at the beach.

- Include **visuals** such as:

Labels

Captions

Diagrams

Photographs

Sequence Chart

Your explanation could have...

a Contents page

CONTENTS

an Index

Index

Some reports also have a Glossary.

Guide Notes

Title: Between the Flags
Stage: Advanced Fluency
Text Form: Informational Report
Approach: Guided Reading
Processes: Thinking Critically, Exploring Language, Processing Information
Written and Visual Focus: Captions, Labels, Index, Photographs, Diagrams, Sequence Chart, Contents Page

THINKING CRITICALLY

(sample questions)

Before Reading – Establishing Prior Knowledge

- What do you know about safety at the beach and the role of lifeguards and lifesavers?

Visualising the Text Content

- What might you expect to see in this book?
- What form of writing do you think will be used by the author?
- Look at the Contents page and Index. Encourage the students to think about the information and make predictions about the text content.

After Reading – Interpreting the Text

- What do you think is the purpose of this book?
- How does the introduction text on pages 2–3 explain the idea behind the topic?
- What inferences can you make about the kind of people who would make good lifeguards and lifesavers?
- Why do you think lifeguards are paid and lifesavers work as volunteers? What inferences can you make about this?
- How does the diagram on page 9 help the reader understand rips and how to get out of them?
- What advantages do you think a lifeguard up a tower has over a lifeguard on the beach?
- What do you think might be involved in a lifeguard's training course for public safety?
- Do you think it is important for lifeguards to learn CPR techniques? Why or why not?
- How did the diagram on page 13 help the reader understand CPR? What other way could you present the information?
- What inferences can you make about why some people ignore water safety rules?
- What questions do you have after reading the text?
- Do you think the author effectively conveyed the information in this book? Why or why not?
- Who would you recommend this book to and why?

EXPLORING LANGUAGE

Terminology

Photograph credits, diagram, index, ISBN number, contents page, glossary, sequence chart